Explode The Code® 2nd Edition 4½

Phonics review and reinforcement

Nancy Hall • Rena Price

Do you get angry...

when a big, frisky puppy...

jumps on you?

Nope!

EDUCATORS PUBLISHING SERVICE
Cambridge and Toronto

Cover art: Hugh Price
Text illustrations: Andrew Mockler, Ann Iosa

Printed in Mayfield, PA, in July 2020
ISBN 978-0-8388-7812-5

6 7 8 9 PAH 24 23 22 21 20

CONTENTS

Lesson 1

When a word has 2 consonants that come between 2 vowels, the word is divided into syllables between the 2 consonants — vc/cv.

trum / pet

Draw a line between the syllables in each word below.

bon|net	object
absent	connect
chapter	wisdom
publish	plastic
expect	droplet

Read, write, and ◯ it.

Word			
lesson lesson	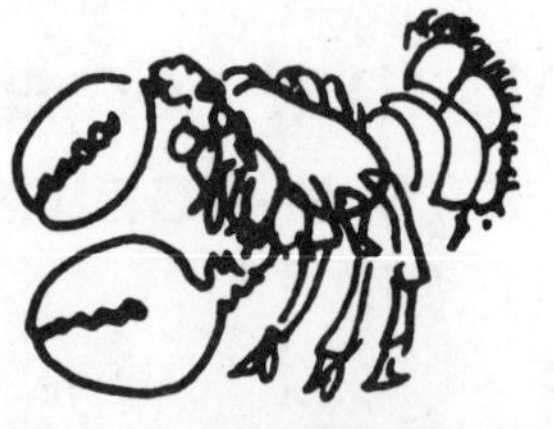	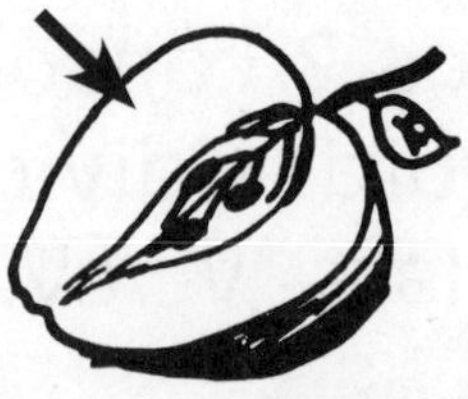	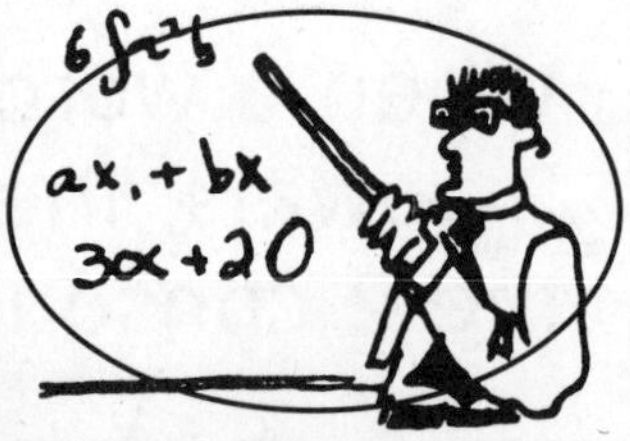
gallop __________	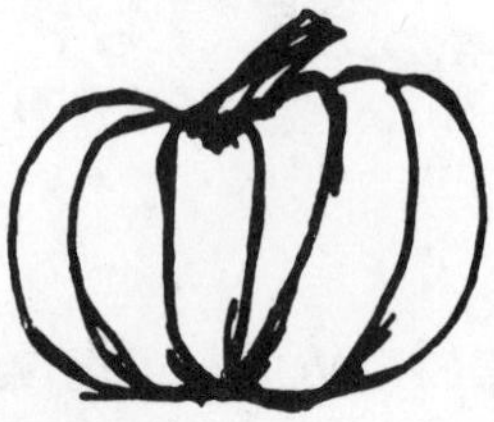	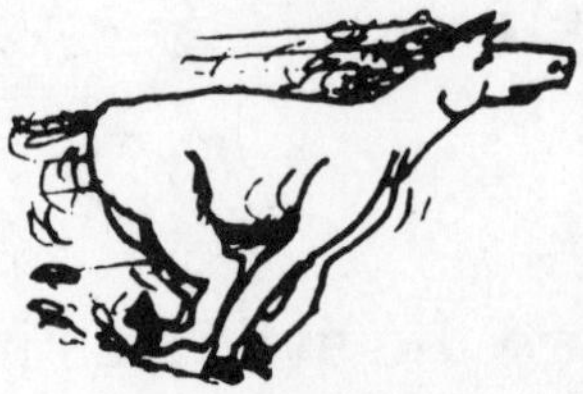	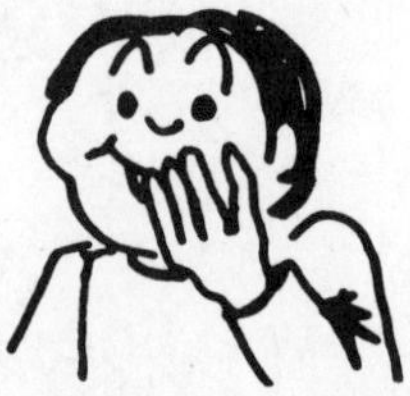
pretzel __________	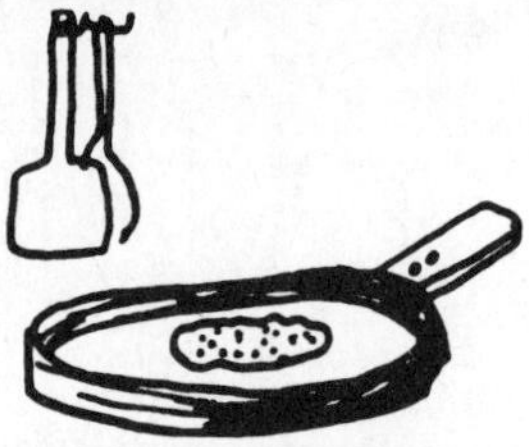	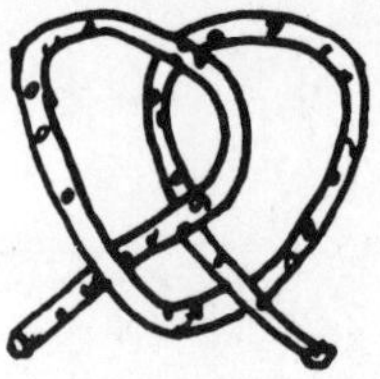	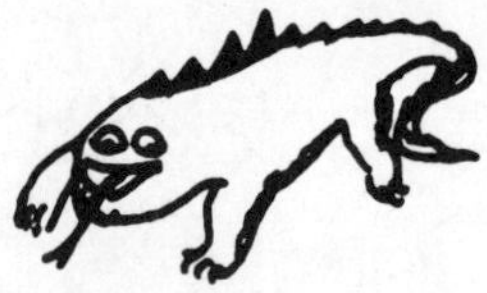
rubbish __________	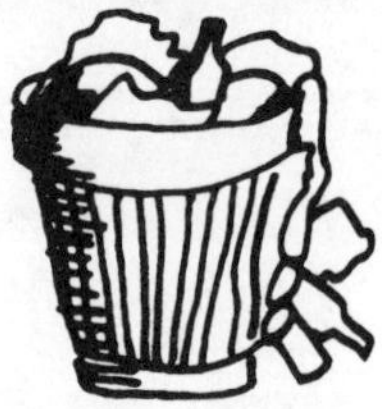	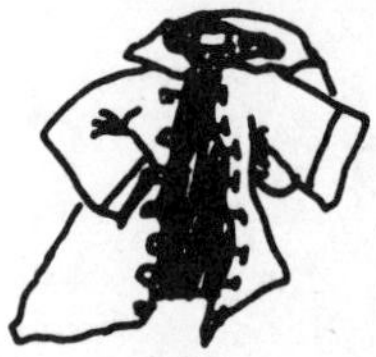	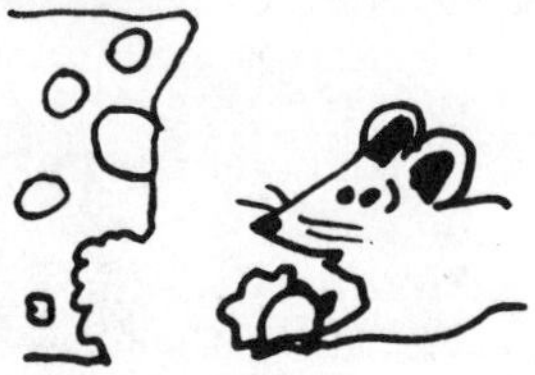
blossom __________	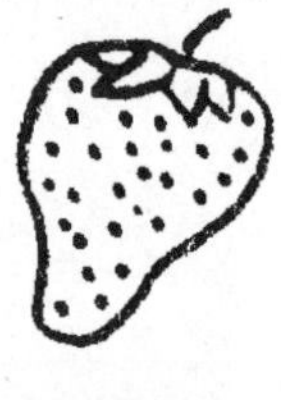	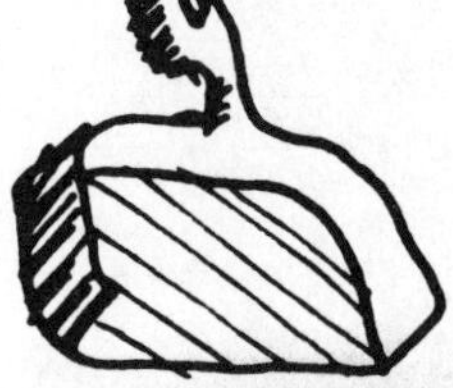	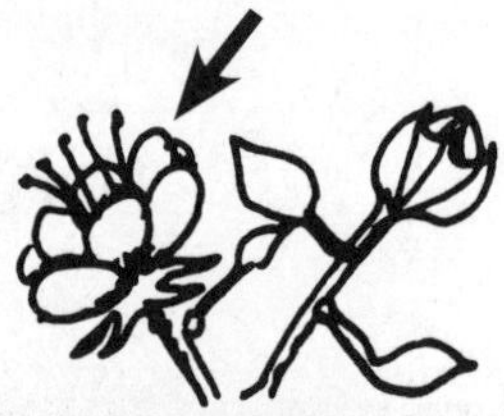
helmet __________	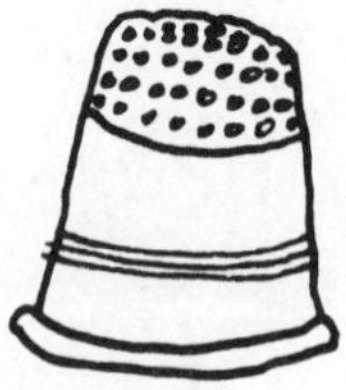	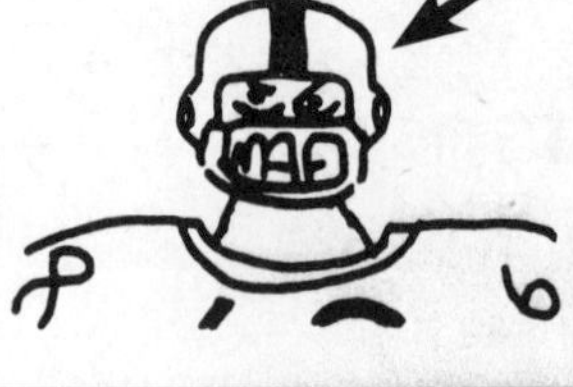	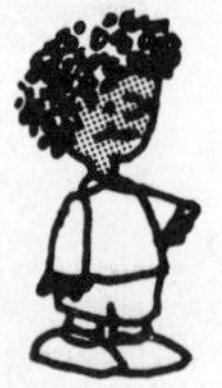
album __________	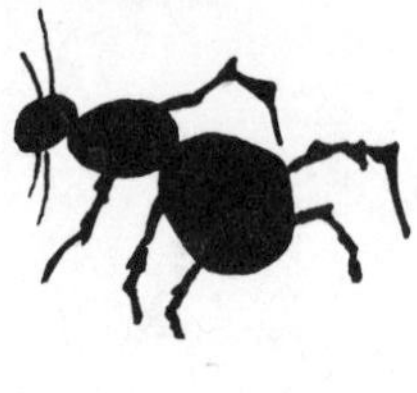	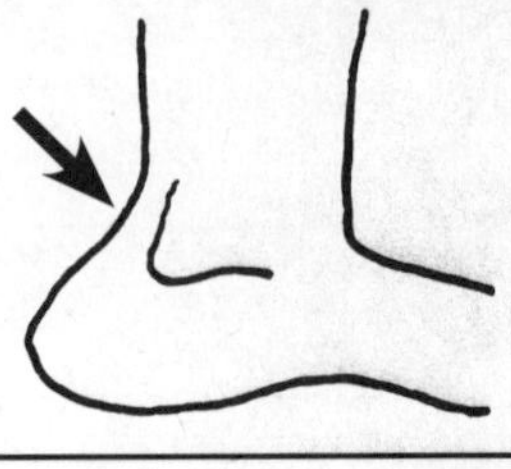	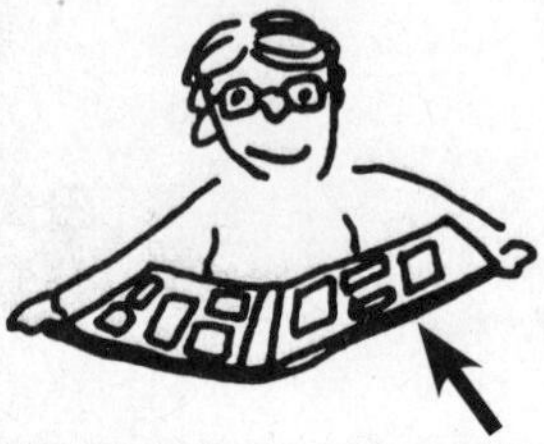

When a word has 2 consonants that come between 2 vowels, the word is divided into syllables between the 2 consonants — vc/cv.

trum / pet

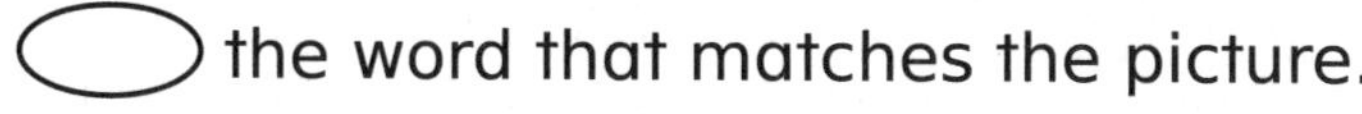
the word that matches the picture.

whiskers or whisper?	tunnel or tomcat?
pepper or better?	contest or connect?
blossom or blister?	padlock or piglet?
tipping or temper?	bottom or button?

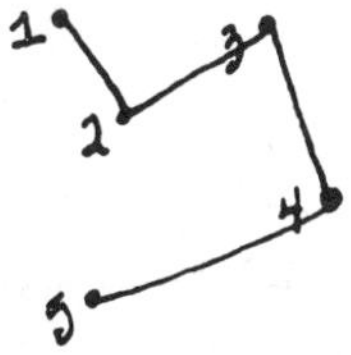

	Spell.				Write.
	(gal)	lag	lap	(lop)	gallop
	dot	bot	mot	tom	______
	in	im	sect	test	______
	pop	pep	per	pen	______
	al	at	dum	bum	______
	cac	cag	tus	sut	______
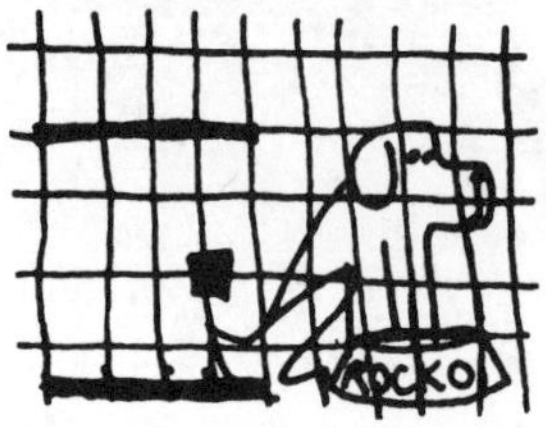	kim	ken	mal	nel	______

Yes or no?

	Yes	No
Can an insect fly as fast as a jet?	☐	☒
Do you like to munch on a pretzel?	☐	☐
Will she need a helmet to play with a kitten?	☐	☐
Can a ribbon be put on a box top?	☐	☐
Would you like to eat a cactus for supper?	☐	☐
Does pepper help a blossom grow?	☐	☐
Should they pick up rubbish after the picnic?	☐	☐

To help read these words, think of the rules to divide words into syllables.

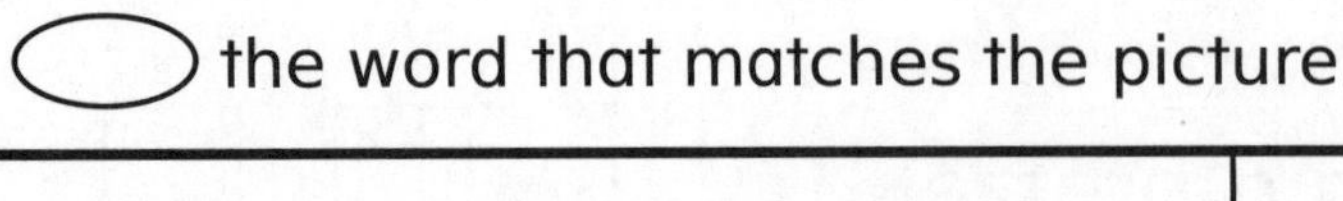

the word that matches the picture.

triplets (trumpet) drummer	whether whisker whisper
hamlet helmet helper	blossom bottom box top
invent insult invite	catnip catsup cactus
kettle kennel nickel	unsafe impact insect

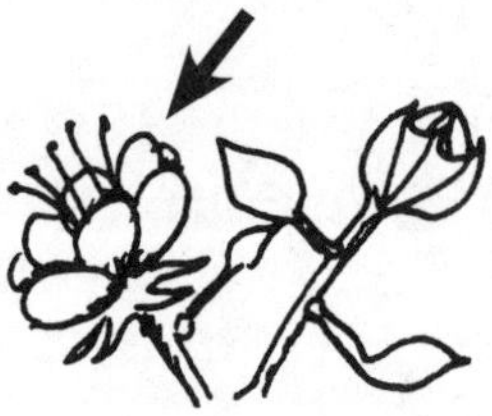

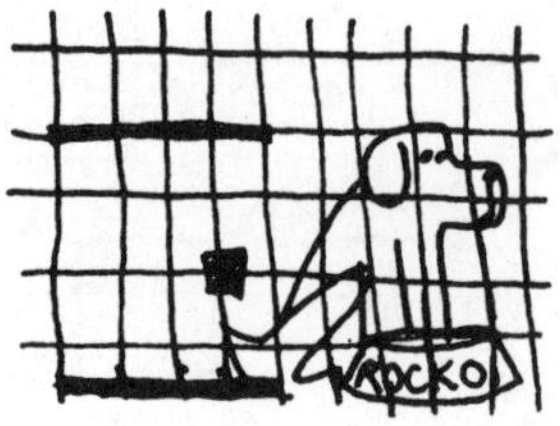

Pick the best word to finish each sentence.

lesson	gallop	~~bottom~~
album	insects	helmet
kennel	whisper	cactus

A box has a top and a bottom .

Lots of dogs can stay in a ________________ .

If you grab a ________________, it may prick you.

The class will try to do a ________________ each day.

He should use a ________________ when he rides his bike on the street.

A bee, a fly, and an ant are ________________ .

Deb likes to ride and ________________ fast on her mare.

X it.

The drummer has a temper tantrum.	☐	
The drummer plays the silver trumpet.	☒	
The tomcat dives for the pretzel.	☐	
The tomcat drives with a helmet.	☐	
Pepper whines in his kennel.	☐	
The padlock on the kennel is rusted.	☐	
The insect sits in the bottom of the glass.	☐	
Ellen inspects the glass-bottomed boat.	☐	
Dot dumps the old album in the rubbish.	☐	
Dot hates to take her old rocker to the dump.	☐	
The rabbit whispers its plan to the cactus.	☐	
The rabbit's whiskers tickle the catfish.	☐	
The monster is singing for its supper.	☐	
My sister acts like a monster when she is swimming.	☐	

Write it.

	helmet

Lesson 2

When 1 consonant stands between 2 vowels, the word is usually divided after the first vowel — v/cv. The first syllable is open, and the vowel says its name.

hō / tĕl

Draw a line between the syllables so that the first vowel says it name.

lilac	crisis
event	locate
spoken	depend
prefer	shaving
elect	pretend

Read, write, and ◯ it.

Friday _______________	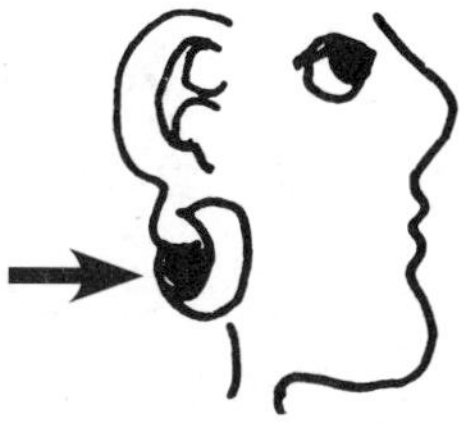		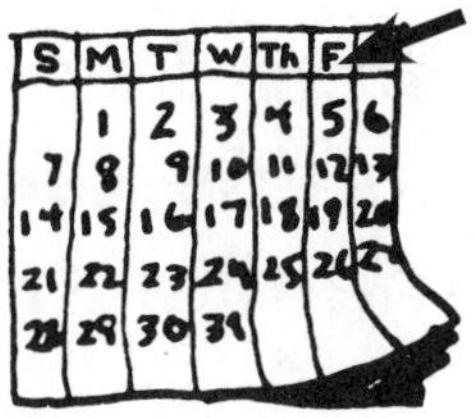
siren _______________			
begin _______________			
Cupid _______________			
hero _______________		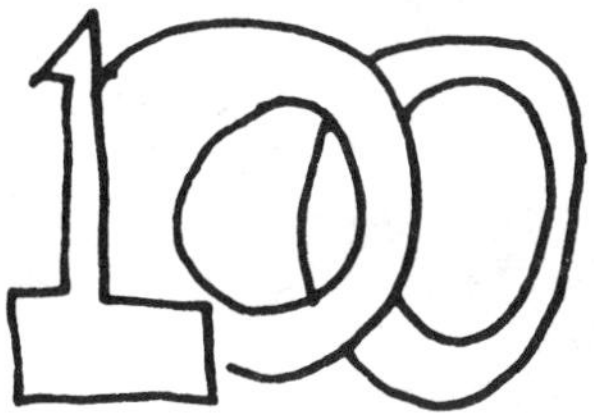	
spider _______________	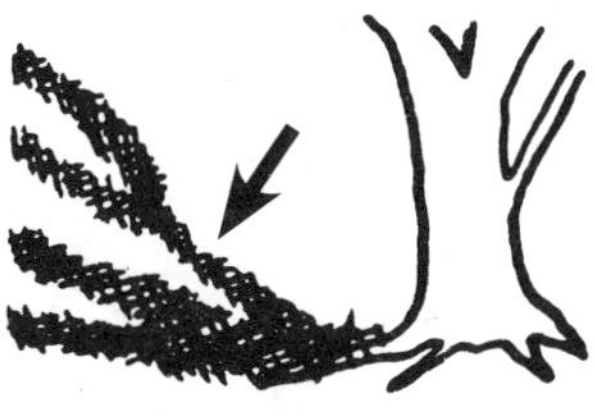		
driver _______________	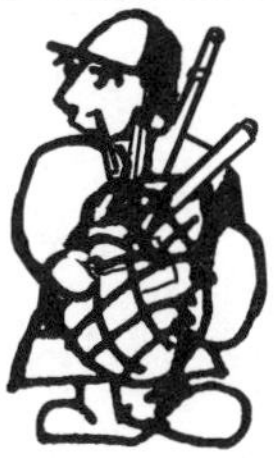		

When 1 consonant stands between 2 vowels, the word is usually divided after the first vowel — v/cv. The first syllable is open, and the vowel says its name.

hō / tĕl

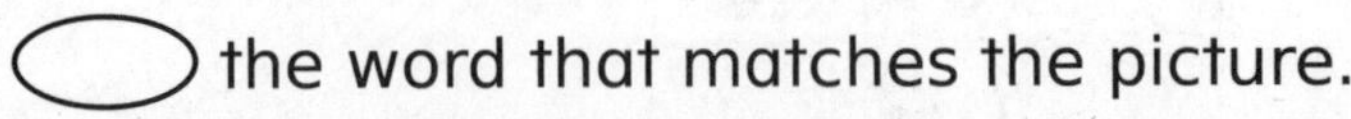 the word that matches the picture.

 beaver or fever?	 hello or halo?
 demo or demand?	 relax or relay?
 omit or over?	 hemlock or hero?
 solo or sofa?	 trading or frozen?

	Spell.		Write.
	sip spi	per der	________
	ha na	to lo	________
	cov clo	ver ner	________
	pap pu	al pil	________
	ba da	sin um	________
	o a	pam pen	________
	sin si	ren ner	________

Yes or no?

	Yes	No
Can you relax and sleep late on Friday?	☐	☐
If you have a fever, do you feel frozen?	☐	☐
Will a driver go faster when she hears a siren?	☐	☐
Will you have good luck if you find a 4-leaf clover?	☐	☐
Is it fun for a pupil to begin Explode The Code?	☐	☐
Does Cupid have a bow and arrow?	☐	☐
If you are a hero, will you have a halo?	☐	☐

To help read these words, think of the rules to divide words into syllables.

 the word that matches the picture.

even
oval
open

finest
Friday
frozen

hotel
motor
hating

silent
silo
siren

demand
David
Danish

basin
basal
basis

consent
clatter
clover

hello
halo
haven

Pick the best word to finish each sentence.

Friday	open	clover
begin	relax	hotel
hero	basin	siren

If he helps save a life, he is a ________________ .

In the grass you may find green ________________ .

I use soap to clean my hands in the ________________ .

________________ is a day that comes each week.

It is fun to ________________ and chat with a pal.

On a trip you may stop and sleep at a ________________ .

You close a gate if you do not want it ________________ .

X it.

The spider will relax and swing in its hammock. ☐ Miss Muffet thinks the spider is a hero. ☐	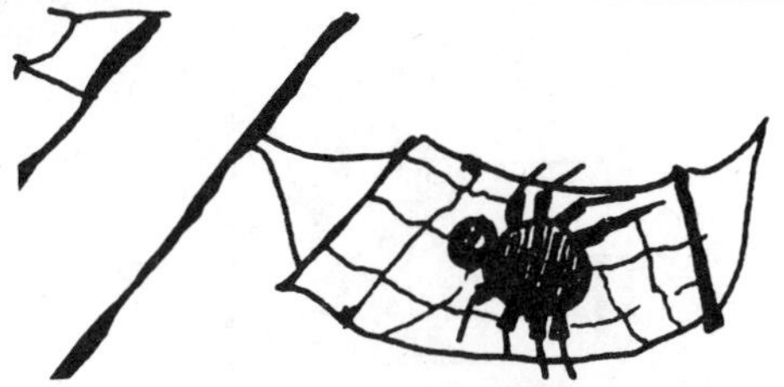
David will open the can and feed Simon. ☐ Simon invites David over on Friday. ☐	
Cupid is picking clover in the grass. ☐ Clover is sticking to Cupid's bow. ☐	
The driver stopped when the siren began. ☐ I pretend there is a siren on my motorbike. ☐	
Susan demands a frozen treat on the hot day. ☐ Susan's feet are frozen in her sandals. ☐	
The pupil with the fever must stay in bed. ☐ Hazel will see if the insect has a fever. ☐	
Jake is singing solo at the hotel. ☐ Jane is washing in the basin at the hotel. ☐	

Write it.

HOTEL	______
	______
	______
	______
	______
S M T W Th F 1 2 3 4 5 6 7 8 9 10 11 12 13 14 15 16 17 18 19 20 21 22 23 24 25 26 27 28 29 30 31	______
	______

Lesson 3

When a word has 1 consonant between 2 vowels, sometimes the word is divided after the consonant — vc/v. The first syllable is closed, and the vowel is short.

rŏb / in

Draw a line between the syllables so that the first vowel is short.

exact	panel
habit	credit
famish	satin
modest	sliver
topic	denim

Read, write, and ◯ it.

camel ________			
dozen ________			
timid ________			
closet ________			
exit ________			
comet ________			
visit ________			

When a word has 1 consonant between 2 vowels, sometimes the word is divided after the consonant — vc/v. The first syllable is closed, and the vowel is short.

rŏb / in

◯ the word that matches the picture.

 travel or gravel?	 over or oven?
 rebel or pedal?	 frolic or frozen?
 tonic or talent?	 sliver or shiver?
 timid or limit?	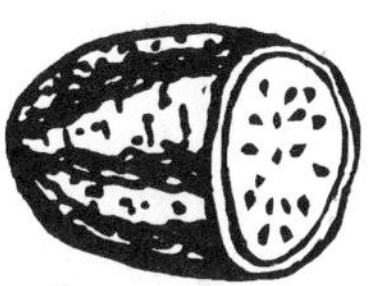 venom or melon?

Spell. Write.

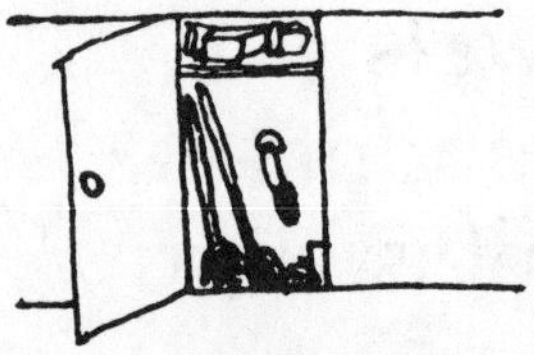	com clos	el et	___
	vis vit	sor it	___
	sic sec	nod ond	___
	ok ex	it at	___
	riv rim	en er	___
	rab rad	ding ish	___
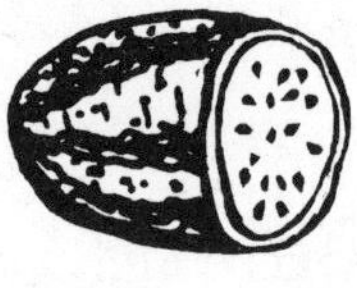	mel nal	on am	___

Yes or no?

	Yes	No
Would you like to eat a dozen melons?	☐	☐
Do robins visit us in the spring?	☐	☐
Is it clever to pedal your bike in the mud?	☐	☐
If you can make a model train, do you have talent?	☐	☐
When you shiver in bed, should you pull up the covers?	☐	☐
Would you mix gravel with pudding and put it in the oven?	☐	☐
If there is a fire, will you go to the nearest exit?	☐	☐

To help read these words, think of the rules to divide words into syllables.

 the word that matches the picture.

camel
clever
closet

secret
second
seven

robot
roping
robin

shiver
shaving
sliver

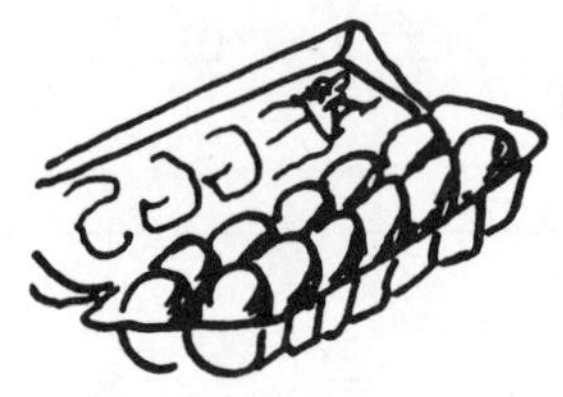

doses
dozen
dozing

clover
comet
cover

topaz
tropics
trapeze

river
rival
rover

Pick the best word to finish each sentence.

talent	visit	radish
oven	model	river
gravel	dozen	cover

When you make a road, you may need ________________ .

David puts a ________________ on top of the pot.

Twelve eggs make a ________________ .

When you bake a cake, you put it in an ________________ .

She likes to row the boat down the ________________ .

Is it fun to ________________ a pal at her home?

I like to put together a ________________ of a plane.

X it.

A dozen kids are on the bus when it has a flat. The bus driver has a dozen eggs in the backseat.	☐ ☐	
Jane has a talent for making models. Jane has a talent for growing melons.	☐ ☐	
The robin shivers as it waits for spring to begin. The robin shaves his beard before spring begins.	☐ ☐	
The river has lots of gravel on its bottom. Rover put lots of grated cheese on his meatballs.	☐ ☐	
Duke will cover the melon with green soap. Grease from the oven covers Duke's pants.	☐ ☐	
The timid robin hopped over to the exit. The clever robin hoped to sneak past the cat.	☐ ☐	
Mabel hit the gas pedal and drove into the bike shop. When Mabel's bike tipped over, the pedal hit the gravel.	☐ ☐	

26

Write it.

Lesson 4

Each of these words has 1 consonant between 2 vowels.

1. If you divide after the first vowel, that vowel says its name:

   pī / lot

2. If you divide after the consonant, the vowel is short:

   prĕs / ent

Draw a line between the syllables in each word below.

linen	moment
mimic	banish
lemon	result
crisis	menu
limit	evil

Read, write, and ◯ it.

Word			
fever ____________			
label ____________			
sliver ____________			
Jason ____________	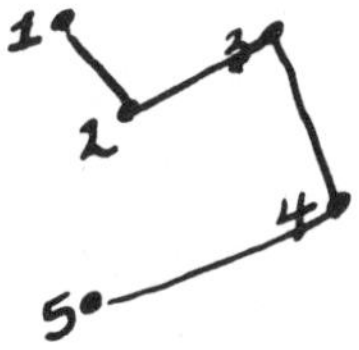		
menu ____________			
shiver ____________			
solid ____________			

Each of these words has 1 consonant between 2 vowels.

1. If you divide after the first vowel, that vowel says its name:

   pī / lot

2. If you divide after the consonant, the vowel is short:

   prĕs / ent

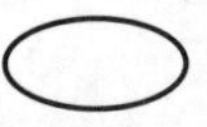 the word that matches the picture.

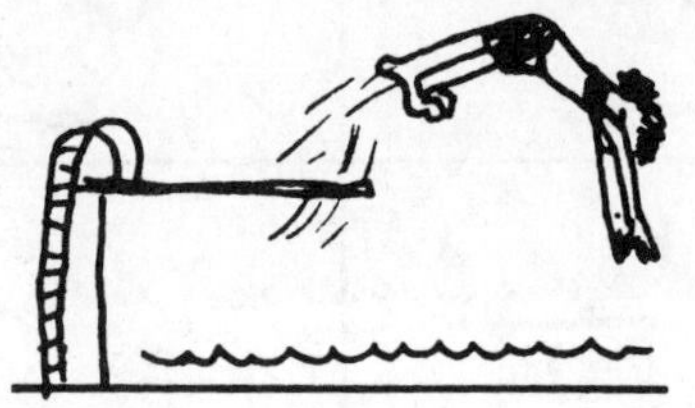 fever or diver?	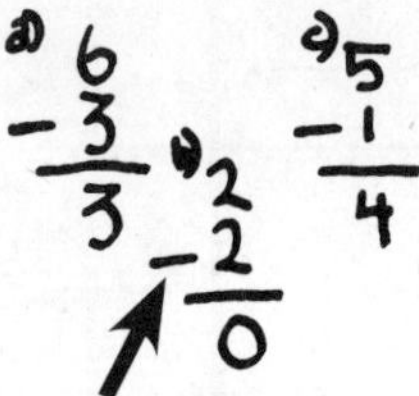 minute or minus?
 blushes or blemish?	 salad or solid?
 rapids or radish?	 banker or baker?
 planter or planet?	 level or liver?

	Spell.		Write.
	pla plan	ent et	______
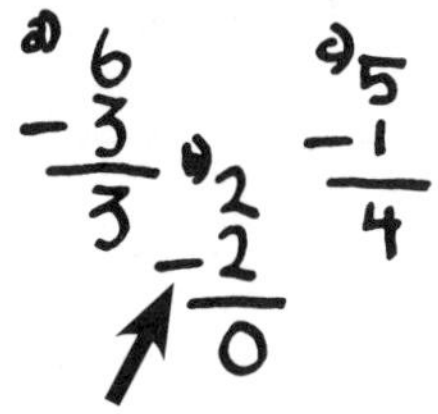	min mi	ute nus	______
	rel rol	ick ish	______
	si sil	lent late	______
	rap rag	ide ids	______
	sliv sil	er ent	______
	ran ra	zor ven	______

Yes or no?

	Yes	No
Do you put relish on a hot dog?	☐	☐
Would a raven make a good pilot?	☐	☐
Is a diver a rapid swimmer?	☐	☐
Will you cry if you have a sliver in your finger?	☐	☐
Have you ever been to the planet Venus?	☐	☐
Do you like waving to trucks as you ride by?	☐	☐
Is it fun baking a cake as a present for a pal?	☐	☐

To help read these words, think of the rules to divide words into syllables.

 the word that matches the picture.

 pilot prevent present	 sofa solo soda
 silent silken sliver	 total pillow pilot
 relax relish relent	 raven radish naval
 waving wasting wrestling	 Chinese chapel chopper

Pick the best word to finish each sentence.

raven	planet	present
silent	minus	chapel
relish	pilot	rapid

When you grow up, you may be a ________________ and fly a jet.

If you can be ________________ when you hide, you may win at hide-and-seek.

They like to grill hot dogs and put ________________ on them.

Do you think someone will discover a new ________________ in space?

A ________________ is black like a crow and can fly.

It is fun to get a ________________ in the mail.

You may get the prize if you are a ________________ runner.

X it.

The diver got a lobster stuck in his mask.	☐	
The lobster is diving deeper into the reef.	☐	
The raven flaps its wings when it visits the river.	☐	
Rachel's raven-black hair blows in the silent wind.	☐	
Jason needs a level cup of milk for his baking.	☐	
Waving her helmet, the pilot lands on the planet.	☐	
Lin got a sliver in her finger chopping the tree.	☐	
The silver ring on Lin's finger was a present.	☐	
Two minus three is seven.	☐	
Ten-three-seven are my padlock numbers.	☐	
The king's wedding was held in the silver chapel.	☐	
That chap had his wedding on a sand dune.	☐	
Rufus has a blemish on his nose.	☐	
Rufus likes relish on his hot dog.	☐	

Write it.

Lesson 5

Sometimes a word has a silent-*e* syllable. If it is at the beginning of the word, divide the word after the silent *e*.

rose / bud

Draw a line between the syllables in each word below.

confuse	volume
empire	homesick
compete	stampede
pavement	locate
provide	suppose

Read, write, and ⬭ it.

tadpole __________			
erase __________		44 x	OUT
polite __________			
umpire __________			
rosebud __________			
campsite __________			
classmate __________			

Sometimes a word has a silent-*e* syllable.

rose / bud

 the word that matches the picture.

 fireside or firehose?	 program or profile?
 trombone or backbone?	 rotate or reptile?
 combine or collide?	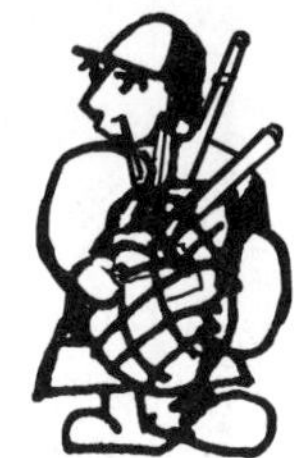 bedside or bagpipe?
 flagpole or tadpole?	 compute or compare?

Spell. Write.

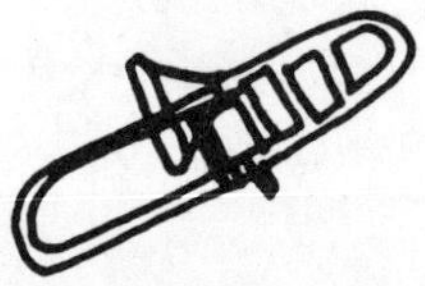	tom trom	bane bone	______________
	cap camp	site sile	______________
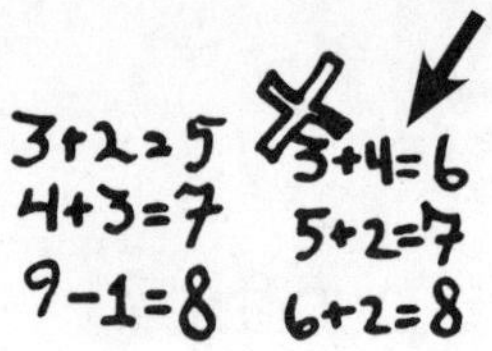 3+2=5 4+3=7 9-1=8 3+4=6 5+2=7 6+2=8	mis nes	tape take	______________
	rose nose	dub bud	______________
	ex es	cape plode	______________
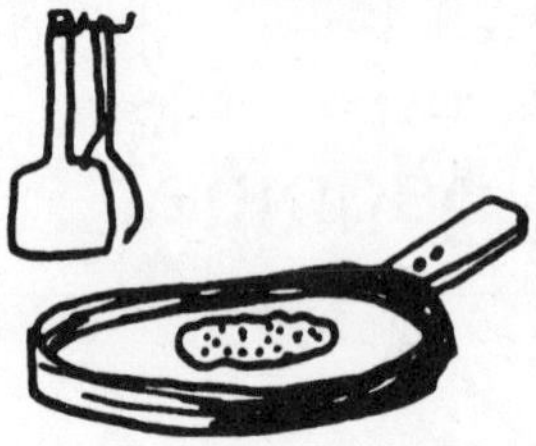	ban pan	cape cake	______________
	in un	side dise	______________

Yes or no?

	Yes	No
If you make a mistake on a trapeze, can you erase it?	☐	☐
Would you put rosebuds inside a closet?	☐	☐
Can you have a bonfire at your campsite?	☐	☐
Is it polite to explode when the umpire calls a strike?	☐	☐
Is it fun to eat pancakes by a campfire at sunrise?	☐	☐
Will a hero use a bagpipe to put out a fire?	☐	☐
Can a tadpole slide down the fire escape?	☐	☐

To help read these words, think of the rules to divide words into syllables.

 the word that matches the picture.

effect
erase
irate

endear
escape
estate

explore
explode
exit

dogtag
backbone
bagpipe

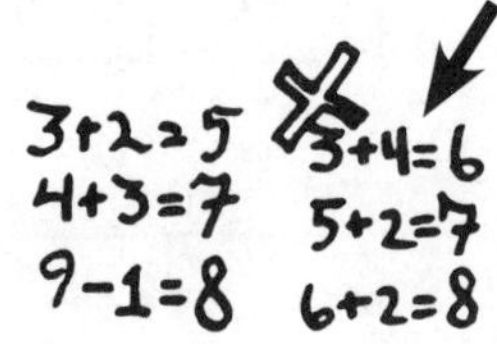

mistake
mistreat
mister

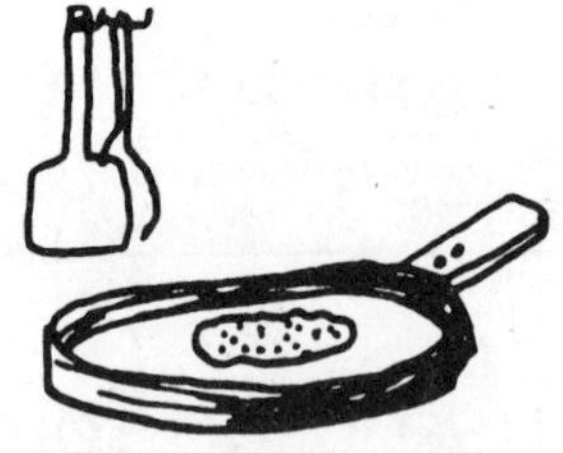

panel
cake pan
pancake

inside
invite
insole

unrest
sunrise
unwise

Pick the best word to finish each sentence.

campsite	trombone	polite
mistake	sunrise	trapeze
pancakes	tadpole	umpire

It is fun to flip __________________ and eat them with bacon.

If you shake hands and say “thank you,” you are __________________ .

I will relax in my tent at the lakeside __________________ .

A __________________ has a long tail and will grow into a frog.

Mabel must use a ladder to reach the __________________ .

At the baseball game the __________________ will say “strike!”

The band makes fine music when LuAnn plays the __________________ .

X it.

The tadpole thinks the reptile is handsome and polite.		
The reptile is the pilot of the big river boat.		
The umpire puts out the campfire at the campsite.		
The camper hides the pancakes by the campfire.		
My classmate makes a mistake when he computes.		
My classmate makes a mistake when he sits on the cactus.		
The rosebud begins to open at sunrise.		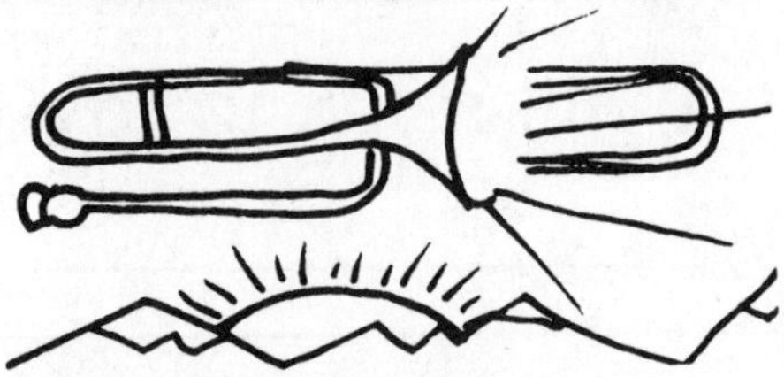
At sunrise the trombone begins to blast.		
The umpire is inside the bullpen.		
The trombone begins to play at sunset.		
Jasper likes to catch tadpoles and put them in a bucket.		
Jasper likes to play table tennis.		
Max Devine gets twisted on the trapeze.		
The trapeze may collide with a firehose.		

Write it.

Lesson 6

Sometimes 2 vowels together in a syllable make 1 sound. This is a vowel digraph syllable: *ai, ay, ee, ea, oa, ow.* The sound is the long sound of the first vowel.

row / boat

◯ the vowel digraph syllables in the words below.

beneath	playtime
painless	hollow
appear	peacock
regain	steamboat
showcase	yellow

Read, write, and ⬭ it.

shadow ____________			
playmate ____________			
teapot ____________			
sneakers ____________			
pillow ____________			
driveway ____________			
stairway ____________			

Sometimes 2 vowels together in a syllable make 1 sound. This is a vowel digraph syllable: *ai, ay, ee, ea, oa, ow.*

row / boat

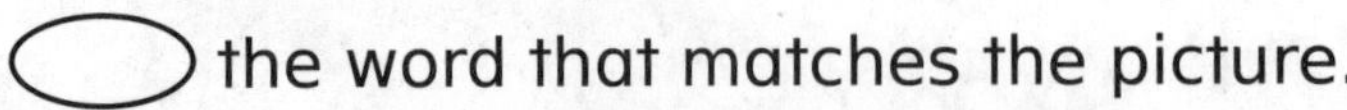
the word that matches the picture.

 teapot or tepee?	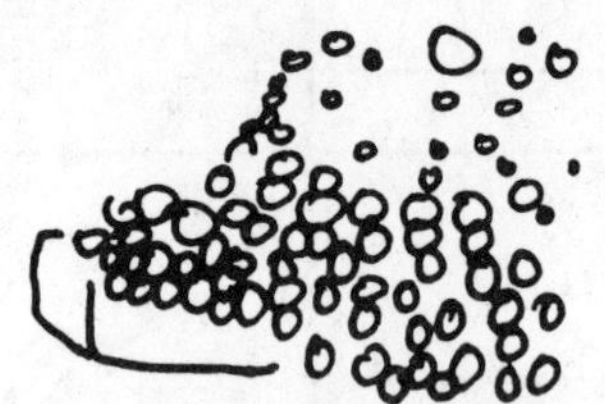 toaster or soapsuds?
 shipboard or skateboard?	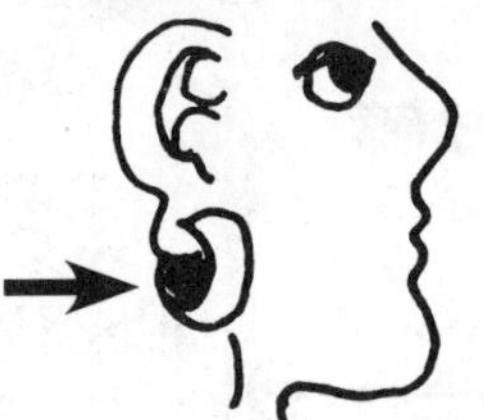 earring or eating?
 cotton or coffee?	 speaking or sneakers?
 beaver or beacon?	 peacock or peanut?

	Spell.		Write.
	rail rain	coat cot	______________
	six sik	ten teen	______________
	bil pil	lay low	______________
	nail mail	box book	______________
	Sun Run	day way	______________
	pai pea	tun nut	______________
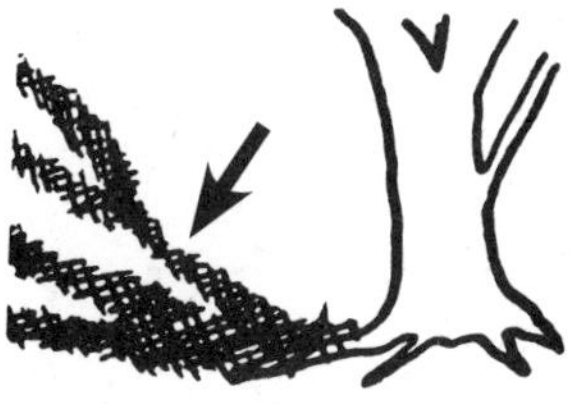	shap shad	ode ow	______________

Yes or no?

	Yes	No
Do you get letters in the mailbox on Sunday?	☐	☐
Should you fill a teapot with soapsuds?	☐	☐
Will you put on your raincoat when you are diving?	☐	☐
Will you and a playmate run up a wide stairway?	☐	☐
Can you feel a peanut that is under your pillow?	☐	☐
When you get in a sailboat, do you put on sneakers?	☐	☐
Do you feel as if you are flying when you step off a stairway?	☐	☐

To help read these words, think of the rules to divide words into syllables.

 the word that matches the picture.

	pillar elbow pillow		mealtime maiden mailbox
	stickpin sixteen seating		steering strainer stairway
	rowboat roadblock roaring		tepee teapot tearful
	playback playmate playpen		spearmint speechless speedboat

Pick the best word to finish each sentence.

teapot	oatmeal	raincoat
peanuts	Sunday	speedboat
pillow	sneakers	shadow

It is fun to take a fast ride in a ________________ .

You should have ________________ on your feet to play tennis.

If it rains, a ________________ can keep you dry.

When the sun shines, the tree has a long ________________ .

________________ comes at the end of the weekend.

At the baseball game it is fun to eat ________________ .

A green blanket and a soft ________________ are on my bed.

X it.

The tepee casts a long shadow at sunset.	☐	
The teapot steams and sings at teatime.	☐	
The speedboat leaves a trail of soapsuds.	☐	
The beaver drives the speedboat with its tail.	☐	
Mabel slides on the stairway rail with a pillow.	☐	
The driver stares at the skunk hidden in Nina's raincoat.	☐	
The umpire heats a teapot at the ball game.	☐	
The umpire heats oatmeal at the campsite.	☐	
Mona has lots of soapsuds in her coffee.	☐	
Milo is spilling coffee all over his raincoat.	☐	
My playmate lost her earring at the Snow Bowl.	☐	
My dad's rowboat is on a trailer in the hallway.	☐	
Pedro is happy to be sixteen years old at last.	☐	
On Sunday six teens played soccer.	☐	

Write it.

Lesson 7

When a word has 3 consonants that come between 2 vowels, look carefully for a consonant blend or a consonant digraph. The blend or digraph will stay together as part of a syllable.

hun / dred

◯ the blend or digraph.
Then draw a line between the syllables in each word below.

impress	hamster
chitchat	instep
reckless	jackpot
backlash	sandman
misspell	unstuck

Read, write, and (circle) it.

dustpan __________			
inspect __________			
pumpkin __________			
nostril __________	90		
tantrum __________			
chopsticks __________			
kingdom __________			

When a word has 3 consonants that come between 2 vowels, look carefully for a consonant blend or a consonant digraph. The blend or digraph will stay together as part of a syllable.

hun / dred

 the word that matches the picture.

 handling or antlers?	 mustang or mattress?
 ticklish or stickpin?	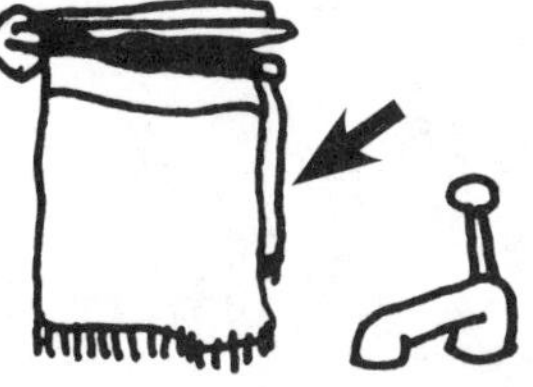 distress or dishcloth?
 desktop or chopsticks?	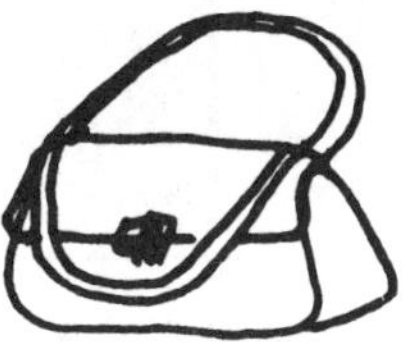 handcuff or handbag?
 snapshot or snapping?	 ketchup or ostrich?

	Spell.		Write.
	dump pump	ling kin	______
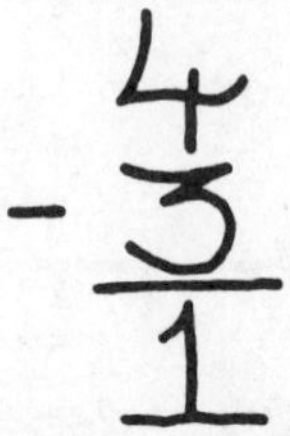	sub bus	tract trot	______
	lad lob	der ster	______
	tin tan	trum drum	______
	nos sun	trail tril	______
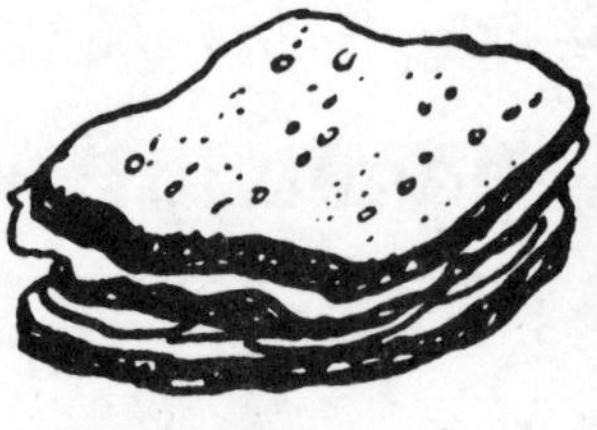	sent sand	wick wich	______
	bang king	dom gun	______

Yes or no?

	Yes	No
Can you cut a smile on a pumpkin with chopsticks?	☐	☐
Does a panther have antlers and a striped tail?	☐	☐
Will an actress pose while you take a snapshot?	☐	☐
Is a lobster ticklish under its nostrils?	☐	☐
Would you dust your nose with a dustpan and wipe it with a dishcloth?	☐	☐
Will your parents be upset if you jump and dive on the best mattress?	☐	☐
Would you have a tantrum if I put a lobster in your handbag?	☐	☐

To help read these words, think of the rules to divide words into syllables.

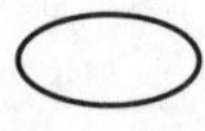 the word that matches the picture.

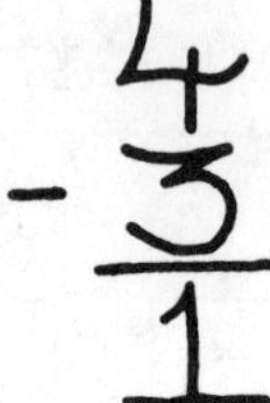	stumble support subtract	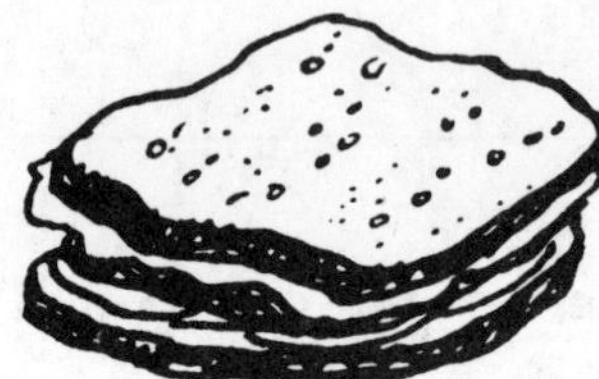	sandman sandwich Spanish
	dustpan dishcloth bluster		endless atlas actress
	huntress hundred hunger	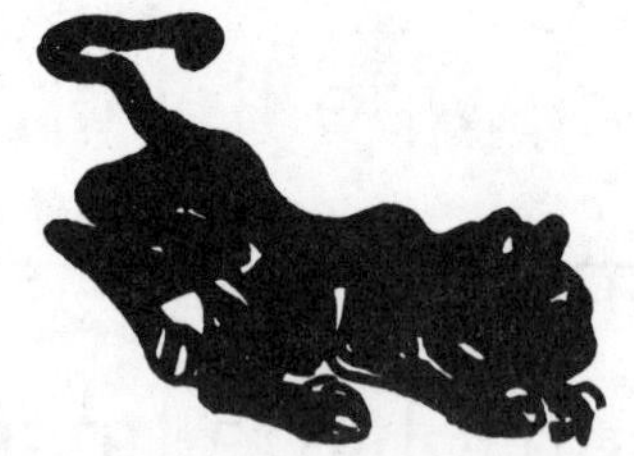	panther banner planter
	matter nuthatch mattress		kingdom ketchup kitchen

Pick the best word to finish each sentence.

chopsticks	kingdom	panther
sandwich	actress	tantrum
mattress	dishpan	pumpkin

If you cut a nose and a grin in a ________________ , you will have a jack-o'-lantern.

When you get mad and cry and stamp your feet, you have a ________________ .

A bed has blankets and a ________________ .

In the tale, the king and queen live in a vast ________________ .

Sally Davis was the best ________________ in the play.

On the picnic we each had a bag of chips and a ________________ to eat.

Jason lets the dishes soak in the ________________ .

X it.

A hundred pumpkins are growing in the kingdom. ☐ The pumpkin became a silver coach fit for a queen. ☐	
The ostrich ate Chester's ham and cheese sandwich. ☐ Chester had a tantrum when his sandbox was broken. ☐	
The buck has its antlers stuck in my handbag. ☐ The duck put handcuffs on the deer's antlers. ☐	
Hilda said, "I can eat a hundred lobsters." ☐ "I am so hot," said the lobster, springing from the pot. ☐	
"Something in this mattress makes me feel ticklish," said Fido. ☐ Matt thinks Fido is ticklish under his chin. ☐	
The panther puts on a kilt when it plays the bagpipes. ☐ The person inspecting the pipes pulls tape from his pocket. ☐	
The actress likes to hear cheering and hundreds of hands clapping. ☐ The endless cheering helped the team push the score to a hundred. ☐	

Write it.

Lesson 8

When you divide a word into syllables, be sure to keep blends and digraphs together.

sun / shine  **rain / drop** 

⬭ the blend or digraph and draw a line between the syllables.

complete	steamship
soapstone	lobster
include	wishbone
concrete	teamster
backside	upgrade

Read, write, and ⬭ it.

roadblock _______________			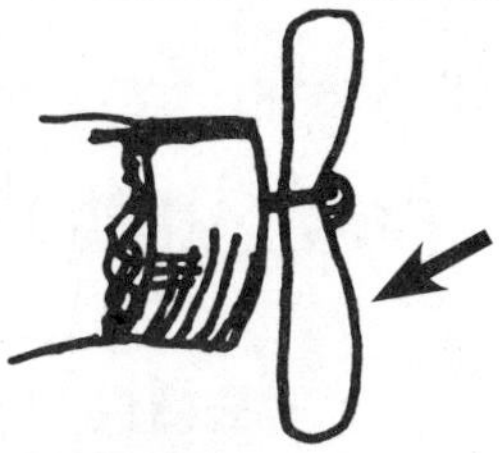
unbraid _______________			
athlete _______________			
complain _______________			 CHICKEN NO REFUNDS
daydream _______________			
nickname _______________	 John Jack Sanderson		 90
bathrobe _______________			

When you divide a word into syllables, be sure to keep blends and digraphs together.

sun / shine **rain / drop**

◯ the word that matches the picture.

showboat or snowflake?

unrest or undress?

toasting or coastline?

backbone or duckbill?

weekday or wheelchair?

raindrop or reclaim?

contain or complain?

milkweed or misspell?

	Spell.		Write.
	leap lap	frog fog	________
	bay day	dream dram	________
	mick nick	home name	________
	ath ash	lete let	________
	ran rain	drop prod	________
	hand had	rail trail	________
	bathe bath	rob robe	________

Yes or no?

	Yes	No
Do you like your own nickname?	☐	☐
Would a milkshake made of milkweed and raindrops taste good?	☐	☐
Can a real frozen snowflake be homemade?	☐	☐
Do you daydream of being a super athlete?	☐	☐
Is a leapfrog a kind of reptile?	☐	☐
Would you complain if we had sunshine all the time?	☐	☐
If you twist your backbone, will you need a wheelchair?	☐	☐

To help read these words, think of the rules to divide words into syllables.

 the word that matches the picture.

	leaflet leafless leapfrog		backward backbone backstop
	unless undress unstuck		stunning sunshine runway
	antler asleep athlete		railroad raindrop rainbow
	cobweb cockroach cockpit		hammock handcuff handmade

Pick the best word to finish each sentence.

handmade	nickname	daydream
backbone	athlete	leapfrog
raindrop	unbraids	handrail

His granddad likes a gift that is ________________ .

My pals like to jump and play ________________ on the grass.

Lee is a fine ________________ and helps win the football game.

If the steps are steep, you can grab the ________________ .

After a swim, Freda ________________ her hair, brushes it, and lets it dry.

It is fun to relax on the grass and ________________ .

Her name is Susan, but Sue is her ________________ .

X it.

Ivan complains of a pain in his backbone. ☐ It is plain that a cactus has no backbone! ☐	
Lulu buys a paintbrush at the store. ☐ Lulu named her new rowboat "Paintbrush." ☐	
Ramon includes Rocko in the Sunday dinner. ☐ Rocko takes a steamboat trip to East Hampton. ☐	
The wise athlete must complete the Latin exam. ☐ The boastful athlete will compete for the grandest prize. ☐	
Winston plays leapfrog with the handbag. ☐ The frog leaped over the handrail and landed on Winston. ☐	
As Thelma daydreams, an oak leaf falls into her milkshake. ☐ It is a mistake for Thelma to daydream of cupcakes and donuts in class. ☐	
Wilma unbraids her long hair and gathers it in a ribbon. ☐ Wilma unbraids the ribbons on her long, satin bathrobe. ☐	

Write it.

Lesson 9

When a 2-syllable word ends in *y*, the *y* says /ē/. The *y* takes the consonant before it to make the last syllable.

pen / ny

Draw a line between the syllables in each word below.

silly	bony
Betsy	creamy
slimy	pansy
dusty	bulky
daily	gravy

Read, write, and ◯ it.

messy ____________			
smoky ____________			
frisky ____________			
rainy ____________			
sixty ____________			
shiny ____________			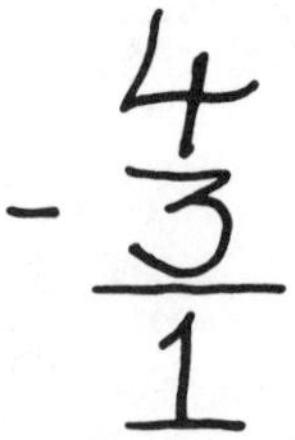
sleepy ____________		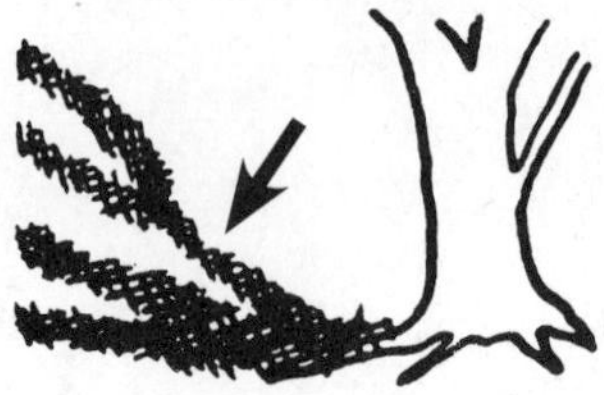	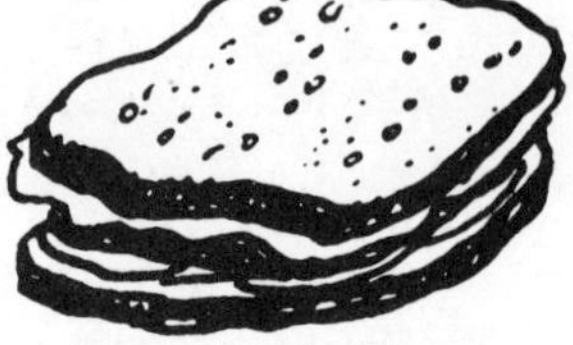

When a 2-syllable word ends in *y*, the *y* says /ē/. The *y* takes the consonant before it to make the last syllable.

pen / ny

◯ the word that matches the picture.

 bunny or bumpy?	 smoky or snaky?
 shaky or shady?	 stuffy or sloppy?
 baggy or Patsy?	 fancy or ratty?
 shiny or shady?	 misty or sixty?

	Spell.		Write.
	mes mus	sy ky	______________
	sow slow	ly gly	______________
	fan fun	my ny	______________
	nine nin	try ty	______________
	sha shab	dy by	______________
	can skin	ny dy	______________
	lad la	by dy	______________

Yes or no?

	Yes	No
Would a penny buy sixty sticks of candy?	☐	☐
Do you get angry when a big, frisky puppy jumps on you?	☐	☐
Can a skinny pony be plump?	☐	☐
If you are ninety years old, are you just a kid?	☐	☐
Would a smoky kitchen make you sneeze?	☐	☐
Do you move slowly when you are sleepy?	☐	☐
Can a weeping willow tree really weep?	☐	☐

To help read these words, think of the rules to divide words into syllables.

 the word that matches the picture.

nineteen
nasty
ninety

pansy
penny
pony

lazy
landing
lady

funny
bony
tummy

navy
rainy
nearest

antlers
angry
annual

slinky
sixty
misty

sleepy
flaky
creepy

Pick the best word to finish each sentence.

shady	frisky	skinny
slowly	rainy	smoky
messy	Henry	sleepy

Hank is one of the nicknames for ________________ .

It is wise to go to bed when you feel ________________ .

The rug was ________________ after the puppy spilled the can of paint on it.

If you feel hot in the summer, sit in a ________________ spot under the tree.

That pony likes to gallop and act very ________________ .

If the wind blows near the grill, the fire may get ________________ .

The sun rarely shines on a ________________ day.

X it.

Patsy is a sloppy eater and drinker.	☐	
Patsy the dragon eats paste and drinks fire.	☐	
Lucky Henry has a shiny red wagon.	☐	
Henry is wagging his shiny red tail.	☐	
The clown has a bumpy nose and funny reddish hair.	☐	
The funny red radish is long, skinny, and bumpy.	☐	
The messy pigs play leapfrog on a rainy day.	☐	
The sleepy pigs complain to the skinny reptile.	☐	
Dobbin, my pony, is sloppy when he eats his dinner.	☐	
The sloppy waiter makes the diners quite messy.	☐	
It was so rainy that Ricky jogged in his swimming trunks.	☐	
Ramon is swinging from the end of a shiny rainbow.	☐	
Lilly became sleepy reading under the leafy tree.	☐	
The weeping willow tree is angry that it cannot weep.	☐	

Write it.

60	________________
	________________
	________________
	________________
	________________
90	________________
	________________

Lesson 10

When *-le* is at the end of a word, it takes the consonant before it to make the last syllable.

cat / tle

Draw a line between the syllables in each word below.

crumble	battle
title	trample
gamble	maple
feeble	simple
smuggle	twinkle

Read, write, and [oval] it.

thimble __________			
table __________			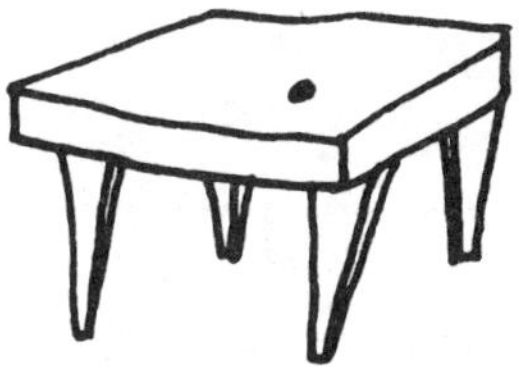
bundle __________			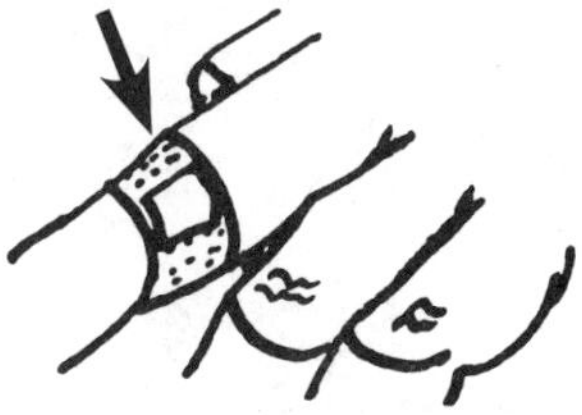
puddle __________		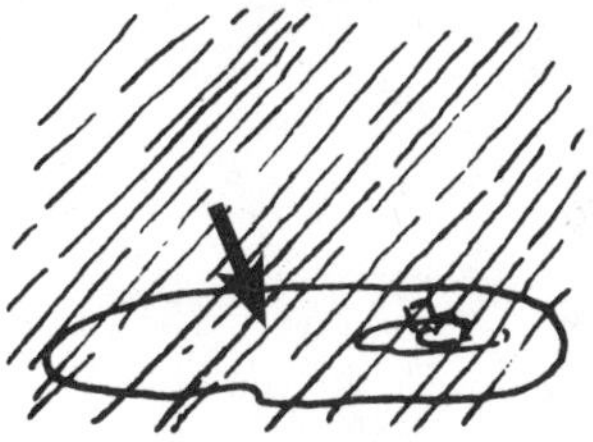	
needle __________		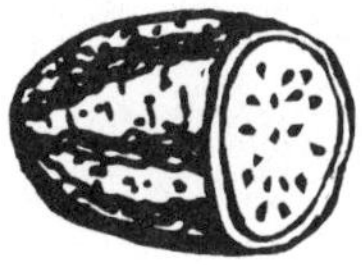	
bubble __________			
stumble __________	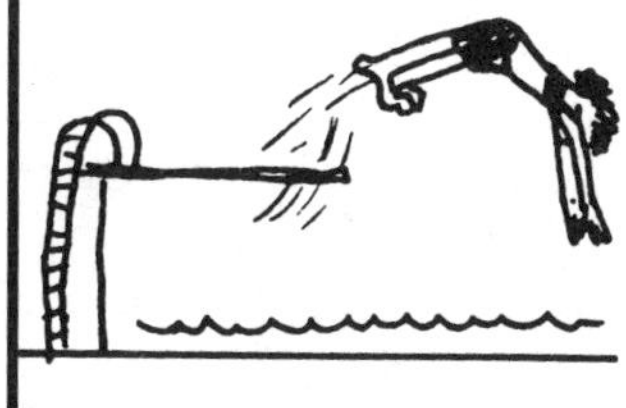	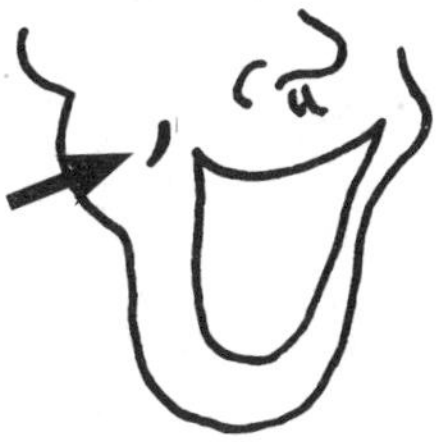	

When *-le* is at the end of a word, it takes the consonant before it to make the last syllable.

cat / tle

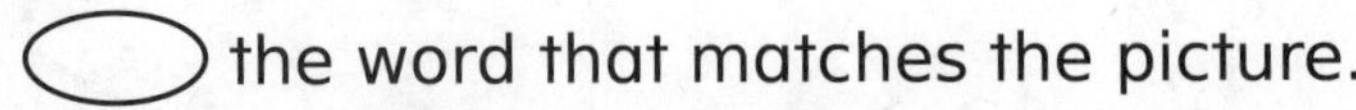
the word that matches the picture.

staple or steeple?	title or idle?
saddle or dazzle?	simple or pimple?
giggle or jungle?	maple or staple?
dangle or ankle?	bundle or fumble?

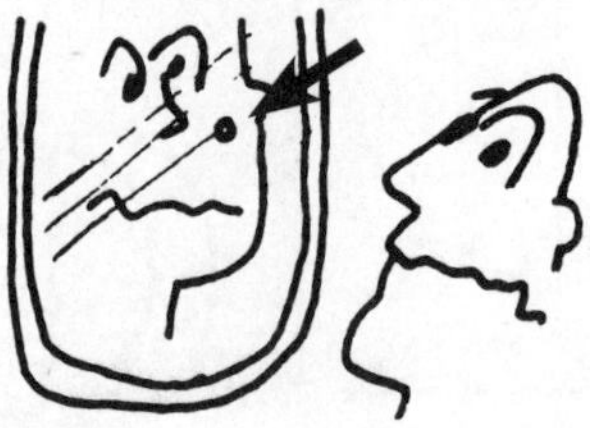

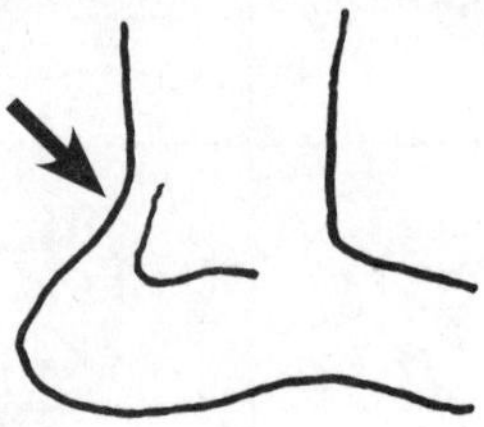

	Spell.				Write.
	ta	fa	dle	ble	________
	sta	dim	ple	ble	________
	im	an	gle	kle	________
	fid	fib	dle	tle	________
	stee	stum	ble	ple	________
	sat	sta	tle	ble	________
	nib	nip	ble	gle	________

Yes or no?

	Yes	No
Do cattle nibble grass in the summer?	☐	☐
If you stumble on the path, will you giggle?	☐	☐
Can you mend a hole in a kettle with a needle and thimble?	☐	☐
Could you put a bridle on a pony in the stable?	☐	☐
Can you twist your ankle when you jump over a puddle?	☐	☐
Would it be easy to put an apple on the top of a steeple?	☐	☐
Is a dimple the same as a pimple?	☐	☐

To help read these words, think of the rules to divide words into syllables.

 the word that matches the picture.

 steeple stumble stable	 tingle little title
 saddle cattle rattle	 kettle kitten settle
 noble needle beetle	 fibber table fiddle
 stable sample staple	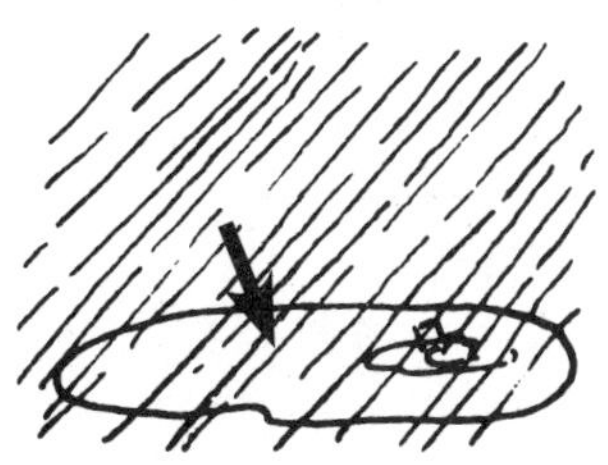 puddle paddle bulge

Pick the best word to finish each sentence.

bridle	needle	title
nibble	bundle	fiddle
ankle	kettle	cattle

She can play music on the ________________ .

You can use a ________________ to help fix a rip.

I heat water in a ________________ on the stove.

Ann rides the pony with a saddle and a ________________ .

Your ________________ may swell if you fall and twist it.

In the pasture I can see sheep and ________________ .

All of the letters in the mailbox are in a ________________ .

X it.

The cattle are drinking from a puddle. Robin likes to drink pudding from the kettle.	☐ ☐	
Tony is playing the fiddle at the table. Tony fiddles with his program during the play.	☐ ☐	
The tiny flea nibbles at Mona's ankle. Mona nibbles on soggy crackers and cheese.	☐ ☐	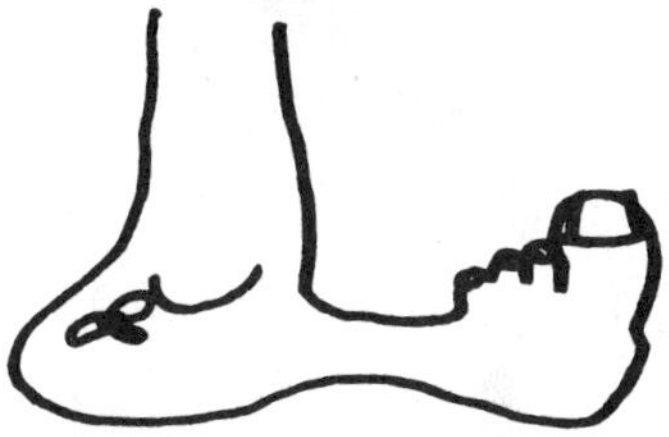
The pony gets a bundle of hay in the stable. The camels take the bundles to the stable.	☐ ☐	
The eagle spreads its wings. The eagle blows a bubble.	☐ ☐	
Betty smuggles secrets to the navy. Betty snuggles into the soft, navy sofa.	☐ ☐	
Ricky giggles as he begins to read the simple lines. Ricky cannot juggle a single apple with a peach.	☐ ☐	

Write it.

Lesson 11

Using the rules you have learned, draw a line between the syllables in each word below.

bad / min / ton

Draw a line between the syllables in each word below.

Atlantic	educate
chickadee	president
rapidly	fiddlesticks
attendant	Mexico
molasses	republic

Read, write, and ◯ it.

monument ______	 90		
buttonhole ______		 HOTEL	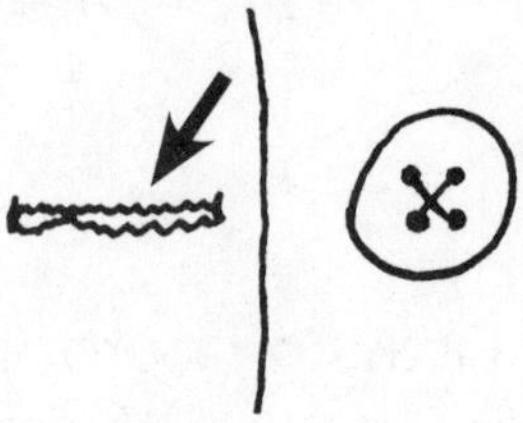
jellyfish ______	 MA'S HOM PEAC		 DING DONG
consonants ______		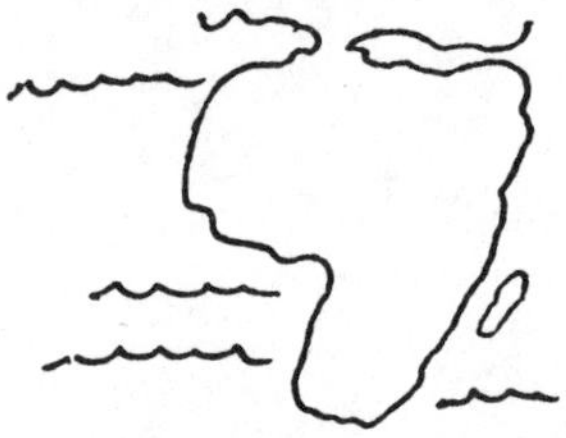	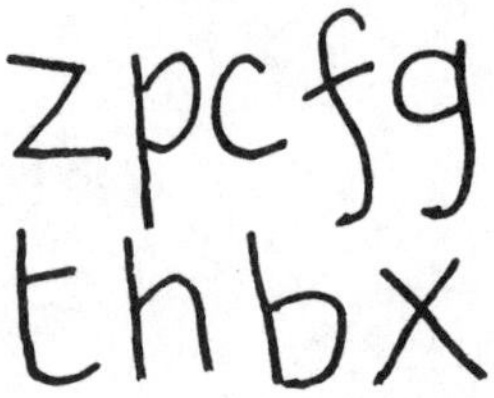 zpcfg thbx
refreshment ______			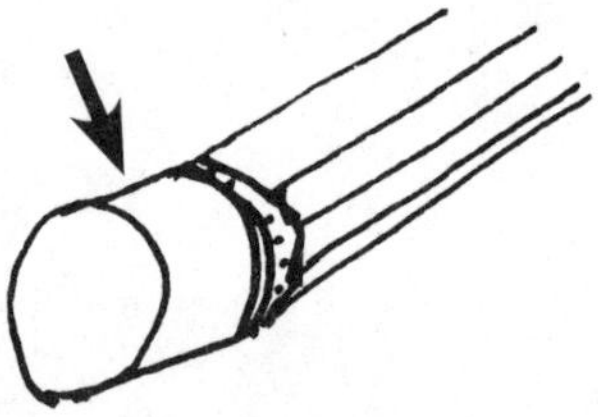
microscope ______	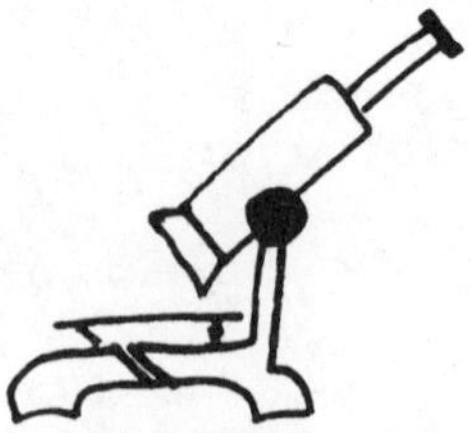	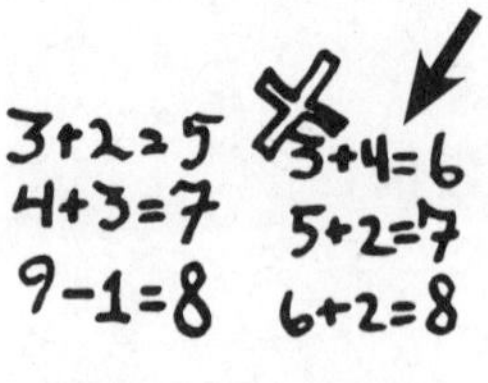 3+2=5 4+3=7 9-1=8 3+4=6 5+2=7 6+2=8	
wintertime ______			

Remember the rules for dividing words into syllables.

bad / min / ton

◯ the word that matches the picture.

 storekeeper or stonecutter?	 unbraided or umbrella?
 evergreen or volunteer?	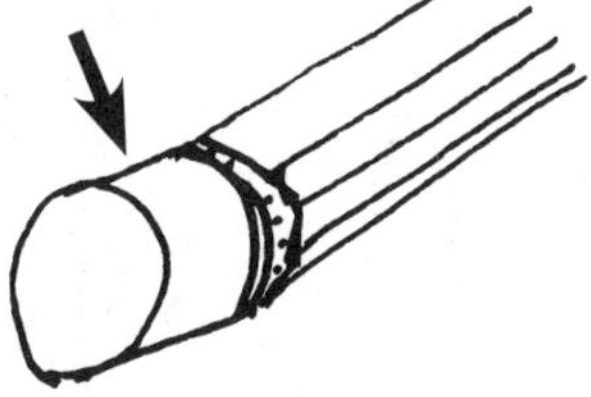 propeller or eraser?
 eleven or elastic?	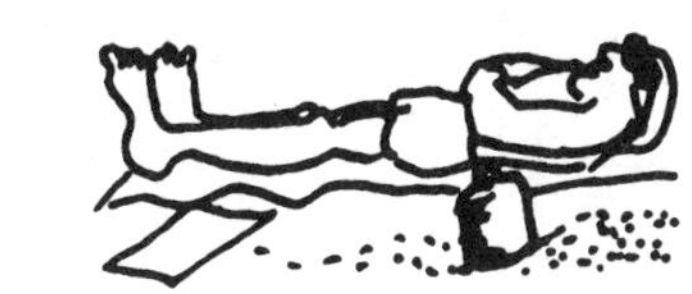 suddenly or sunbathing?
 confident or monument?	 pineapple or penmanship?

	Spell.			Write.
11	e al	lev le	en wen	____________
zpcfg thbx	con co	so con	ex nants	____________
	pin pine	ip ap	ple ble	____________
	win wi	ter der	tim time	____________
	bag bad	min mut	ton tone	____________
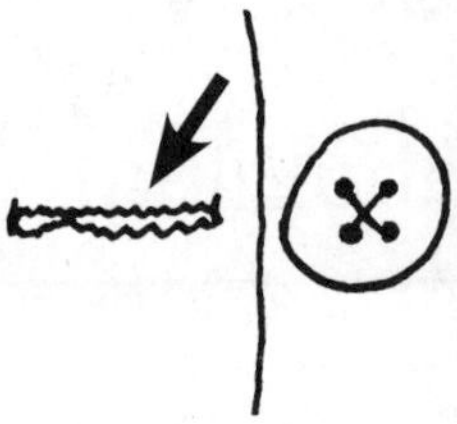	but bu	ton gun	hole hall	____________
	le lem	none on	ade ad	____________

Yes or no?

	Yes	No
Is it fun to play badminton with an athlete?	☐	☐
Do you get vitamins from your daily meals?	☐	☐
Are there seven consonants in *peppermint?*	☐	☐
Will you discover a jellyfish while skating in the wintertime?	☐	☐
If you are sunbathing, are you beginning to get a tan?	☐	☐
Would you volunteer to clean the erasers?	☐	☐
Do you make lemonade with a pineapple?	☐	☐

To help read these words, think of the rules to divide words into syllables.

◯ the word that matches the picture.

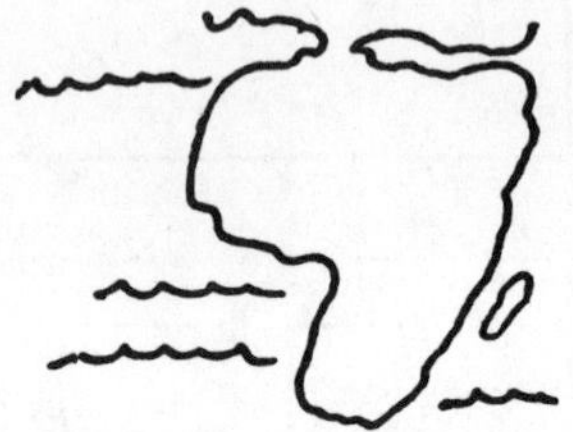	commander commenting continent		summertime seventeen suddenly
	pillowcase pocketbook pineapple		volunteer venison volcano
	president peppermint popular	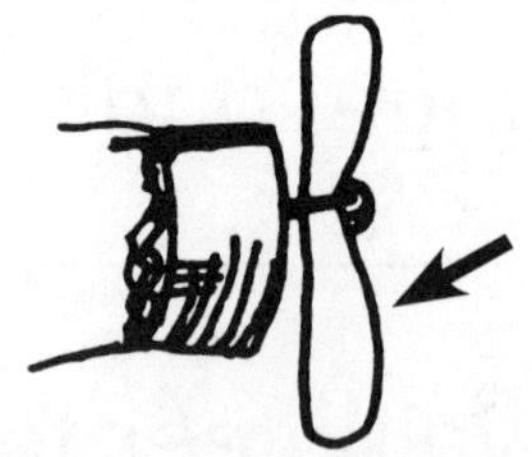	probably propeller provided
	lemonade melody paperback		backgammon banister badminton

Pick the best word to finish each sentence.

lemonade	wintertime	volunteer
consonants	peppermint	continent
jellyfish	microscope	buttonhole

The letters, not including *a, e, i, o,* and *u,* are called __________________ .

With a globe you can study each sea and each __________________ .

A __________________ will make a tiny thing seem big.

Do you like to make snowmen or ride on a sled in the __________________?

On a jacket each button fits in a __________________ .

After I mow the grass and get hot, I drink some __________________ .

A stick of red and white candy may taste of __________________ .

X it.

The inventor is poking his finger into his sneaker.	☐	
The insect is sneaking under the broken microscope.	☐	
The jellyfish is sunbathing on the sandy beach.	☐	
The clever sunfish is making beach plum jelly.	☐	
A dozen pineapples doze under a shiny umbrella.	☐	
Pamela does not understand that pineapples will not make lemonade.	☐	
The propeller on the small plane is quite shaky.	☐	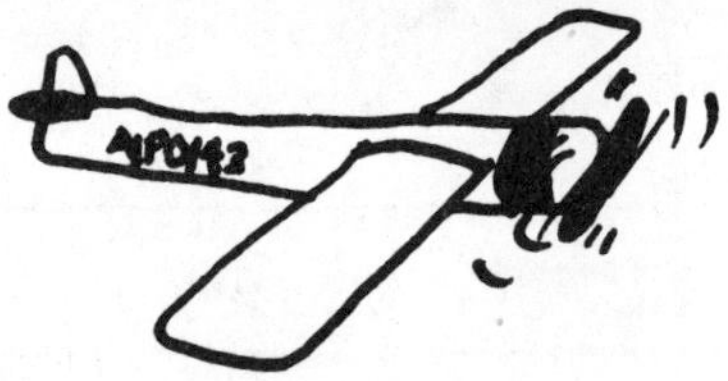
The shaky glider has no propeller.	☐	
Seventeen pupils volunteer to clean the erasers.	☐	
The pupils see the volcano erupt seventeen times.	☐	
Felix has a chocolate hat and a peppermint cane.	☐	
Felix bakes a chocolate cake with peppermint frosting.	☐	
The band stopped to salute at the monument.	☐	
The bandit traveled across the frozen continent.	☐	

Write it.

	____________________
	____________________
	____________________
	____________________
	____________________
	____________________
	____________________

Book 4½ — Posttest

(Teacher dictated. See Key for Books 1 to 5.)

(circle) the word you hear.

1. slipper silver sliver silken	2. animal actress antlers athlete
3. compare complain compact compute	4. bunchy bumpy dumpy dusty
5. crabbed crayon crater credit	6. robot relate rotate rebate
7. sample simple ramble sandal	8. profits frolics tropics trapeze
9. propeller professor prosecute protector	10. volume valentine volunteer voluntary

Book 4½ — Posttest

(Teacher dictated. See Key for Books 1 to 5.)

1. ______________________________

____

2. ______________________________

____

3. ______________________________

____

4. ______________________________

____

5. ______________________________

____

Using the rules you have learned, put a line between the syllables in the words below, and mark the vowel in the first syllable long or short.

relax	railroad	tempest	helpful
crazy	dictate	fellow	jackpot
title	begin	madness	infect
thimble	hamster	sprinkle	minus
ugly	distress	spinach	mistake
choppy	driveway	insult	sunrise
basin	riddle	reason	relish
public	profit	belong	weekend
rainbow	holy	tantrum	finish
stampede	fable	beneath	handful
suspend	comic	nostril	locate

Use the words to complete the sentences.

athlete	sneakers	ankle	slowly
puddle	bundle	rainy	relax

1. If you can jog five miles, you are a real __________________ . You don't need much equipment, but you do need __________________ that fit well. You begin by running __________________ and then you go faster. Even if it is snowy or __________________ , you keep on running. But do not splash in a __________________ ! Remember that when you get home you can sit and __________________ .

teapot	raindrops	table	pineapple
chopsticks	menu	ticklish	China

2. When we go out for a Chinese dinner, we sit at a __________________ and read the __________________ . We select the chicken with __________________ and lobster with peapods. We eat the meal with __________________ . The waiter brings a __________________ filled with hot tea. Would it be fun to live in __________________ and eat this way every day?

Go on to the next page.

stingray	butterfly	river	erase
driveway	rowboat	diver	appears

3. Molly is rowing on the ________________ when she sees a dragonfly. As she takes her ________________ net to try to catch it, she tumbles from the ________________ into the water. The shadows of the seaweed scare Molly. "Will I be attacked by a ________________ or a jellyfish?" she wonders, but no sea monster ________________ . Molly swims safely to shore, and then she tells her Dad, "I will never be an undersea ________________ .